My Phoenix Rising
Poetry Compilation

Christina Saldon

Contents

Acknowledgment i

About the Author ii

Reunion 1

Apology From the Past 2

Empathy's Plight 3

Letter to My Demons 4

Letter to My Demons – Part 2 5

Loss 7

Introspective Thought 8

Identity Crisis 9

A Complicated Mind 10

Societal Dilemma 11

We Will Remember 12

Thanks for Being You 13

Trauma's Voice to the Aggressor 15

Friendship Found 16

The Barefoot Queen 17

My Grandmother 18

A Day of Remembrance 19

Girls Trip 20

Echoes From the Plantation 21

Gratitude's Verse 22

Love Unrequited 23

Self Outing 24

A Child's Trauma – An Adult's Healing 25

Self-Recrimination 26

First True Love 27

Learning to Love Again 28

Healthy Relationship...29

Life's Simple Joys 31

Grace...32

Because I'm worth the fight...34

Where I am Meant to be...36

Dating Social Media Style...38

It is Okay to not be Okay...39

Trauma's Journey 41

A Child's Trauma Memory...42

Feelings Journey 43

Music Heals 44

Distance Love Letter...45

My Love...46

Distance Relationship Woes...47

Hope...48

Loyal Friendship 49

Destiny...50

Bad Memories 51

You Can't Save Me 53

Mirror Reframed...54

Perspective...55

The Journey...57

Living with Anxiety 58

Freedom's Ride...59

The Apology...60

Acknowledgment

This compilation of poetry was a labour of love for me and I owe credit to many individuals for rekindling my love of writing. This journey started after my 36-year High School Reunion. I put myself out there to be part of the committee, something that was definitely outside my comfort zone, but by doing so, I was able to receive far more than I gave.

The friendships forged during those formative years were still as strong as they once were, and reliving our memories of one another truly sparked my will to live the best version of my life and to become the best version of myself.

This book has many muses, and I hope they see themselves in the lines of these pages, as there are far too many of you to mention by name.

You will also see moments of self-doubt but also moments of clarity and healing.

May the words contained within provoke thought, emotion and your own healing journey should you require healing.

Life is meant to be lived, and once you cast aside your fears and hate, you will find your own path to your best life.

I truly hope you enjoy reading the poems as much as I have enjoyed writing them.

About the Author

Christina Saldon is from Nova Scotia and has a large family and extended family. Her core values include family, truth, justice, loyalty, duty and sacrifice. She is a veteran of the Canadian Armed Forces and served in the Air Force as a Resource Management Clerk for almost 20 years. The highlight of her military career was a seven-month deployment to the Sinai Peninsula in Egypt. She still works in the Administrative and Finance field, and helping military families is her passion.

Christina is a survivor of childhood and adult trauma and suffers from PTSD and Anxiety disorders. She is a huge supporter of therapy and counselling.

"My greatest wish and hope is that everyone who needs to heal finds someone to help them along that journey, whether it is a friend, a trusted confidant or a healthcare professional. It is important that you find the right fit. If you don't find it initially, keep searching until you do. You are worth the time and the investment." Christina Saldon

Reunion

When we were young

We were carefree

We felt like we had won

All was right for you and me

Then came graduation day

And we went our separate ways

Some of us beginning new lives far away

Time separating us day by day

Years pass, and we lose touch

Memories creep in of glories since past

Then we want to reach out very much

Hoping friendships of the past lasted

Reunion, someone says, let's get together

Anxious at first to see old chums

But once you are there, everything is better

Friends once more, we are the lucky ones

Christina Saldon

Apology From the Past

You've been on my mind since last night

You apologized for a long ago fight

Once you explained your point of view

It was I who should apologize to you

I am sorry my words didn't land right

Sorry they stirred feelings of anger

The scars you bare didn't see the light

I am saddened my words still linger

What I meant and what you heard

Were miles and miles apart

I wish we talked like this back then

But I am glad we get to restart

Empathy's Plight

To feel so deeply

A gift and a curse

Joy so bright

Despair void of light

Joy propels you forward

At the speed of light

Despair weighs you down

Where solace can't be found

Some don't come back

Is it strength I lack

Do I just watch as I fade to black

Or do I fight and claw my way back

Two paths from which to choose

One I win, and one I lose

Perspective determines which is which

Christina Saldon

Letter to My Demons

Hello friend, I see you are still here
Stomping around my heart and soul
Filling me with guilt and shame
In the past, you would wreak havoc

But now I have new weapons
To help keep you at bay
And maybe finally drive you away
I am no longer alone

I have others to help me remember
I am more than the things you tell me
More than the trauma you inflicted
They walk beside me hand in hand

Reminding me of what is real
Providing support and laughter
Providing comfort and love
This gives the strength to banish you again

Goodbye, my old friend
I hope we never meet again
But if we do, I will have the same weapons
To banish you again and see me through

Letter to My Demons - Part 2

I am tired of wearing you like an old shoe

I have worked hard to banish you

Maybe that is my mistake

Maybe I should envelop you in my embrace

When I cast you aside, it doesn't work

You just stand there and smirk

Because you know you will be back again

Back to where it all begins

So it's time to stop this insanity

Time to put an end to my vanity

I won't toss you away

Instead, I will welcome you to stay

Now it is I who wears the smirk

As I begin to realize this will work

Today, I can finally see

You no longer have power over me

Christina Saldon

I look to the sky and the sun

I feel the warmth upon my face

Thoughts flowing like a rhythm drum

Carrying me to my happy place

I see a wooded country lane

With a guitar resting against a large tree

A scene so serene yet plain

A place I feel truly free

Solace I temporarily find in my mind

Loss

Life, Death, Grief

Happiness, Sorrow, Despair

Light fades to dark

Thoughts shift

My soul aches

My resolve falters

Pain wreaks havoc

Responsibility heavy

The weight is crushing

Ultimate escape wanted

But so much left unfinished

Stand, Dust off, Move forward

It is not my time yet

But another is gone forever

Christina Saldon

Introspective Thought

In the dark before the dawn

My mind is silent and free

The sun's rays reflected on the lake

Serenity, enveloped by the calm

As the sun climbs in the day's sky

My mind becomes busy

I yearn for the quiet of pre-dawn

Alas, the day requires my mind's decisions

Then the day comes to an end

The tiredness courses through me

My mind is still racing

Sleep does not come easy

Finally, I fall asleep

Never very deep

Until I wake to the peace of pre-dawn

So it can fuel me to carry on

Identity Crisis

What is it that people see

I am sure it isn't really me

They only see the side I portray

And hear the guarded words I say

Do I personify the traits said

This haunts me as I lay in bed

The armour I wear hides all

The trauma and doubt will be my downfall

Why don't I see what they do

Why do I have a different view

How do I reconcile the two

I am tortured by the inner fight that ensues

What is it that people see

I am sure it isn't really me

Christina Saldon

A Complicated Mind

Forbidden fruit out of reach upon the vine

The turmoil of thoughts and feelings combined

I continue the work to make them unwind

Then I look again to the sky and the sun

I feel the warmth upon my face

I conjure memories full of fun

And I recreate my happy place

Societal Dilemma

The term physical health

Is so widely accepted

Yet the term mental health

Is so viciously disrespected

Why is one considered okay?

While the other is felt in shame

I can't wait for the day

For physical and mental health to be treated the same

Take care of your entire health

Seeking help is not weak

Don't put your mental health on a shelf

Stand up and let your heart and mind speak

Let's look after our entire health

Therein lies our true wealth

Christina Saldon

We Will Remember

This night, we remember

This night, we cherish the fond memories

This night, we see the years that have gone by

This night, we reflect on the present and past

This night, we share stories

This night, we cry and laugh

This night, we remember

This night, we are grateful we can still feel

This night, we honour them by raising a glass

This night, we remember

This night, we realize these memories will last forever

This night and every night, we will remember

Thanks for Being You

In the time it takes a teardrop to roll down my cheek

One kind word from you dries the river of pain from my face

Sometimes, you know how I feel before I feel it myself

You know the way to make things right

Before I spend another sleepless night

Whenever I need a friend, you have always been right there

No matter what it takes, you've always shown you care

I guess what I'm saying is that I truly appreciate

The time that you've given me to make my life complete

In the time it takes a heart to beat

You've always been right there

To dry my tears with laughter

And show how much you care

Some days, I'd never make it

Without you in my life

You're the best thing that's ever happened

To ease my troubled mind

If I believed in Angels

I'd have to say you are mine

God is smiling down on me

I'm glad he found the time

I wrote this poem to tell you

That I care about you, too

And someday, maybe God will let me ban an Angel too

Until then, thanks for being you!

Trauma's Voice to the Aggressor

A life spent living in shame

Because you chose to hurt this child

Robbing me of my innocence

I grew up with an uncontrollable rage

An anger that grew and was wild

When the anger was at bay, I was reticent

For years, I have struggled emotionally

Too ashamed to share my pain

Too confused by the guilt I feel

Now, I am working to understand rationally

That I was not the one to blame

Now I can feel what is real

I was the one who was done wrong

And I had no choice but to be strong

Maybe I should thank you

But that is a cheeky stance

However, I am the better person

And I am now working to be my best version

Christina Saldon

Friendship Found

A friendship that was unexpected

Feelings of being mutually respected

I hear your name, and I smile

To see you, I would travel miles

I enjoy being around you and your company

Whether we are two or many

My face usually hurts from the laughter

They can hear our cackles in the rafters

I grin at the way you slap my back

When amused, you give it a good whack

It is interesting how quickly we connected

Maybe it is our kindness that is reflected

Our friendship was a pleasant surprise

I look forward to all it will provide

The Barefoot Queen

We set sail on the Barefoot Queen
The riverboat showed us an idyllic scene
The banks were lined with gorgeous homes
The history of the waterway felt in our bones

We met some wonderfully nice folks
They listened when we spoke
We laughed, drank, sang and ate
The cruise was of the highest rate

We made friends with Mary and Kenny
Mary shared her story aplenty
Poor Kenny wasn't in the know
But it soon would be the end of the road

Once they were back at home
He would have to go
Why did she share that with us, Canuks
Well, because we are swell, awe-shucks

The Barefoot Queen was full of tales
It was definitely an adventurous sail

Christina Saldon

My Grandmother

There is a woman in my life

Who is strong and kind

Who is wiser than time

She listens when I speak

She keeps things forever in my reach

She sees when I am blind

She makes things easy for me to find

She always knows what to say

She keeps sadness far away

She has seen the world good and bad

No matter what, she is never mad

In my life, she must always be

Because I need her to keep me free

Her love blankets me like no other

If you haven't guessed

She is MY GRANDMOTHER

A Day of Remembrance

One day to honour them seems so inadequate

Those who gave their lives selflessly

Those who served at home and abroad

Those who continue to serve to keep the peace

To protect our rights and freedoms

In the air, on land and at sea

Their struggles should never be forgotten

And know those who survived may have hidden scars

When you rise each day, say a word of thanks

Because without them, you would not have a day to enjoy

Thank you to all who have served

And all who continue to serve or will serve.

We will remember

Christina Saldon

Girls Trip

We set out on a crazy adventure

Driving south to a beach paradise

Ladies considered to be mature

But once there, we were young and pure

Walking through the sand to frolic in the surf

Wasn't long before it was considered our turf

Folks we met were generous and kind

Our new oasis was quite the find

We found activities that strengthened our bond

Time spent together was warm and fond

Three great friends were easy to find

These are the ties that bind

Echoes From the Plantation

We walked through the fields of history

We learned some of their stories

Their lives now less of a mystery

I could feel the weight of their worries

I walked in their steps and felt their darkest days

But I could also feel their spiritual ways

The strength they must have displayed

Allowed me to feel the non-existent sun's rays

Their humanity warmed my soul

But their struggles brought me sadness

The abuses they endured leaving a hole

This world is filled with too much madness

Gratitude's Verse

Thank you, 2023, the year I have reawaken. The year, things became clearer. The year I learned to see my self-worth.

Thank you, 2023, for finally allowing me to be my real self. The year of learning, growth and healing. The year I learned the depths of my true wealth.

I will always remember 2023 because that is when I became the best version of me. Now, I am attracting the people who will help me remain free.

Thank you, 2023, for my greatest gift, the love of another. I didn't believe I would ever feel this type of love. But here we are 2023, so blissfully happy.

Thank you, 2023, the year I finally found me.

Love Unrequited

She is beauty redefined
A soul so pure and kind
I have to love her from a distance
Because I know she'll never be mine
I can only love her in my dreams
A forbidden romance, tender and sweet
A heart full of love so deep
An ache that brings me to my knees
I will only ever love her in my dreams
Our friendship is strong and meaningful
But she will never know how I truly feel
She will never love me the same
I am not who she wants or needs
I can only love her in my dreams
A forbidden romance, tender and sweet
A heart full of love so deep
An ache that brings me to my knees
I will only ever love her in my dreams
I yearn to be close to her
To touch her in a loving way
Loving her from afar will need to be enough
She'll never be able to share this type of love
I can only love her in my dreams
A forbidden romance, tender and sweet
A heart full of love so deep
An ache that brings me to my knees
I will only ever love her in my dreams

Christina Saldon

Self Outing

I have hid myself away

For far too long

Suppressing who I really am

Not allowing myself to be seen

Maybe deep down, I always knew

But fear kept me from being true

Until I finally put myself first

I was unable to acknowledge who I really was

Now I know my true worth

Now I feel I am whole

Fear still grips my heart and soul

Concerned with being accepted

Will friends and family embrace the new me?

Or will they cast me aside

Did they already know and truly see

Time will tell, and what is meant to be will be

A Child's Trauma – An Adult's Healing

Christmas has never been my favourite time of year

It was filled with abuse, fear and anger

Those memories used to make it hard to spread the cheer

I hung onto my anger, treating everyone like strangers

Decades of learned behaviour to overcome

Seeing my family and friends' joy and elation

How do I alter my thinking and the person I've become

Maybe by creating new memories and traditions

So, I vow to find the spirit this holiday brings

To choose family, friends and charity to rise above

The true meaning of Christmas is not more things

But time spent honoring those we love

Christina Saldon

Self-Recrimination

So full of disappointment and anger

I just want to smash the wall

Rage swelling inside me to the point of danger

In my mind, I am curled up in a ball

Tears of anger continue to fall

What is the damn point of it all

Why do all that work seem for nothing

This isn't the life I am wanting

Surrounded by friends who care

But few can truly understand

Sometimes, I wish I existed nowhere

But I must muster my strength at hand

Exhaustion sets in all over

I can't maintain this mental pace

I need to take a beat and breathe slower

To settle my mind to a state of grace

First True Love

When I am happy, it is because I carry your love in my heart and soul.

When I am sad, I picture being in your warm embrace, where I find your love and strength.

When I am angry, I picture your hand on my heart, calming me back to peace.

Your love and light will always guide me back to a state of grace.

If this can happen with the mere thought of you, imagine the power of your physical presence and touch.

You are the love of my life. I give you my heart, my soul, my light and together, we will shine forever bright.

Learning to Love Again

Love sought from another

Deciding to be vulnerable again

Looking for a friend and a lover

Someone who sees the world to be discovered

Looking for our peaceful oasis

One we can enjoy together

A place full of romantic spaces

To show our tenderness no matter the weather

They need to be compassionate and kind

They need to be passionate and funny

They need to value my heart and mind

We would create a world bright and sunny

Love sought from another

I'm looking for a friend and a lover

Healthy Relationship

I awake with thoughts of you

Shining from my soul as bright as the morning sun

Warming me from head to toe

My heart pounding from my thoughts of us

Imagining your touch, the warmth of your embrace,

The softness of your skin, your lips on mine, such sweet kisses

These thoughts fuel me through my day

I smile as you cross through my mind

The stress of the day fades away

Replaced with longing to be with you

Happy imagery reappears in my mind's eye

My mind drifts to my version of our future selves

And I am caught smiling yet again

A smile so wide, so deep, so vibrant

As my day ends, the sun has long since set

Now, my sleepy thoughts are still of you

Thoughts of you lying beside me in our bed

Snuggled as one in a warm embrace

Exchanging kisses and cuddles

Until we both drift off to sleep

This is when I fall deep into my slumber

Wrapped in the most titillating dreams, keeping me until morning

When I awake with thoughts of you

Shining through me as bright as the morning sun

You remain with me every moment of every day

Someday soon, we will be together

And these thoughts will be reality

Beginning our life together filled with love, joy, and happiness

Finally, our thoughts will turn to memories.

Life's Simple Joys

Have you heard the melodic harmony of the birds' daily concerts?

Have you felt the warmth from the noon sun's radiant rays?

Have you seen the majesty of colour from a rainbow after a spring shower?

Have you smelt the fragrances from a vast field's flowers?

Have you tasted the salt on your lips from the ocean's spray?

Have you sensed the presence of a powerful energy and allowed it to envelope you?

Have you accepted love from others after you learned to love yourself?

Have you discovered your worth and felt your own power?

Have you learned to navigate your feelings to cleanse away all the wrong?

Have you caressed the body of someone you love?

Or been held so tight that you lost all feeling?

Learn to listen, look to see, touch to feel, emote to connect and then you will begin to heal.

Grace

Today is a good day for me

Today, I see the sun even through the dreary sky

Today, I feel the warmth even though it is cold outside

But there have been so many days

Where I could not feel the warmth

Even though the sun's rays beamed

And everything was much harder than it seemed

The good days fuel my soul

So, I can weather the days that I feel low

Knowing that this is a moment in time

And not my forever state

Helps me to navigate

Allowing myself the grace to just be

In whatever state I need

To help me take the next step forward

Life is meant to ebb and flow

And good cannot exist without bad

Again, I remember this is a moment in time

And not my forever

My Phoenix Rising

On those good days

I will continue to fill my cup to overflowing

So, it will hydrate me on the ones

That I feel less than

Because this is a moment in time

Not my forever

Christina Saldon

Because I'm worth the fight

I look up to the sky

I look down at the earth

I let the tears flow down my cheeks

And I wonder why I'm still alive

Some days, I cannot rise

From my safe and comfy bed

Some days, I brave the world

Even when I am stuck in my head

I'm drowning in my despair

But I keep fighting that daily fight

Sometimes, I feel I am beyond repair

But I keep holding on real tight

Because I'm worth the fight

I believe the lies my brain weaves

I lean into the pain, wanting to let go

Why, lord, oh why must I suffer so

Wouldn't it be easier if I just let myself go

I'm drowning in my despair

But I keep fighting that daily fight

My Phoenix Rising

Sometimes, I feel I am beyond repair

But I keep holding on real tight

Because I'm worth the fight

Then I put on that familiar smile

And go out into the world

Hiding myself from everyone

Hiding my pain and troubles

I'm drowning in my despair

But I keep fighting that daily fight

Sometimes, I feel I am beyond repair

But I keep holding on real tight

And I will keep holding on tight

Because I'm worth the fight

Christina Saldon

Where I am Meant to be

It's been a long, hard road

But I made it right here, to where you are

I made it over the hills and through the valleys

Through the sunshine and the storms

Through the good days and the bad

Continuing to move forward one step at a time

Searching for myself in the sky and on the ground

In the trees and the ocean and the seas

In the faces of strangers, family and friends

But where I needed to search was in the mirror

And the monster that lives within

The one that shows up when I am low

The one that never knows when it is time to go

Thank God for the road that led me to you

Your love has helped me tame that monster within

Now I have found myself and like looking in the mirror

Seeing myself through your eyes has sparked my self-love

Now, I can be the person I was meant to be

Being loved by you and loving you has set me free

My Phoenix Rising

I am no longer locked in my own hell

I look forward to meeting our days

And working with you to find our way

Life now has new meaning

And the future holds space for big dreams

Now, I embrace all my feelings

Knowing it is worth what is on the other side

It's been a long, hard road

But I made it right here, to where you are

And there is no place I would rather be

Dating Social Media Style

I remember the day you reached out

I was skeptical and full of doubt

Your beauty and youth disarmed me

How could you be interested in the me you see

We speak every day; we have so much to say

I want to know everything about your days

We talk about the past, present and future

I fell in love with your heart and good nature

Your love and support lift me up

You jolted me out of my decades' rut

Your image warms and fuels my thoughts

Our love grows each day; it loosens my heart's knots

Soon, we will meet and be in the same space

Hopefully, we have built a sturdy relationship base

Once together, we will enjoy each other's embrace

Then we will decide where will be our final place

It is Okay to not be Okay

Sometimes, I lose my way

And I know I am not okay

The pain hits me like a storm's wave

Or like a leaf blowing in a hurricane

Some days, I stumble and fall

Some days, I can't climb the walls

I built to protect myself

So, I stay in my pit of fear

There are days I can't people

I just can't maintain control

So I hide myself away

Until I calm my mind and soul

It's okay to not be okay

We all, at times, have lost our way

We all heal in our own way

Through words, nature, music

Or some of us pray

Please hear my words

It is okay to not be okay

Christina Saldon

Remember, it is a moment in time

We can all lose our way

Just remember it is okay to not be okay

As long as it is not your every day

Trauma's Journey

I find comfort in the routine of the mundane

A sense of peace, serenity or solace from my pain

I have stopped trying to outrun it

Instead, I have found a place for it to fit

I now wear the pain like a badge of honour

My battle armour earned as a survivor of lifelong trauma

I no longer languish in the pitying thoughts of 'why me.'

I've replaced them with thoughts of 'It has made me, ME!'

I draw strength from my own resolve

But also from those who have helped me to evolve

Many have accompanied me along my healing path

Many who deserved it have felt my unrestrained wrath

Everything I feel still remains intense

I may be more self-aware, but pain still drives my senses

My body still holds my survival's tension

I keep quiet, feeling things aren't worth it to mention

I have accepted I will always have this daily struggle

But I also know I am strong enough not to crumble

The weight of the past no longer pins me down

I now know my heart and soul are sound

I find comfort in the routine of the mundane

These tasks help to keep me sane

Christina Saldon

A Child's Trauma Memory

I remember the first time I felt fear

I was only three years old

I witnessed the physical abuse of another

Then I experienced the horrors I have never told

I learned at a young age that there would be no saviour

I dreamt of suicide every day and night

I thought that would be the only way to end the abuse

But I was too much of a coward to take that way out

Or was I strong for choosing to go on

It took many years to finally begin to heal

To finally understand I was not to blame

And that I could let go of my misplaced shame

Now I know my worth and my true power

I am not a victim but a survivor

Happiness is now in my grasp

Because I have done the work to come to terms with the past

Feelings Journey

Anger
    Sadness
        Fear
          Shame
I knew them all too well

Frustration
    Blame
        Hate
         Rage
Filled most of my childhood and youthful days

Then like the flip of a switch
    Hope
        Joy
         Love
           Happiness
Crept in and finally my healing could begin

Gratitude
    Forgiveness
        Empathy
         Grace
Helped me to find a much better place

Christina Saldon

Music Heals

Have you felt the power of music and song

Was it the message in the lyrics

Or the guitar solos and riffs

Maybe the drum beats or the cadence

Maybe the vocalist's ability to emote

Or did you feel your own connection

Was it the imagery of the music video

Or the energy of a live performance

Could have been it was easy to sing along

They say music can heal all

I have loved music as far back as I can recall

I truly love it all

The melody

The beat

The message

The energy

And the way it makes me feel

Music will continue to help me heal

Distance Love Letter

Can you feel my love from where you are

Can you hear the tenderness of my words

Can you imagine the pounding of my heart

Can you believe we were born out of the stars

Do you want to feel my arms around your waist

Or my lips upon your face, body and lips

Feel me softly caress your body

Feel my breath upon your face

As I whisper sweetly in your ear

Oh, baby, my love knows no bounds

I want you here with me, always

I want to feel our love for me

I want to hear the tenderness of your whispers

I want to feel the beating of your heart

I want your hands to find their mark

Baby, you can caress my body and face

But first, we need to be in the same place

Christina Saldon

My Love

My love is blissful

My love is kind

My love is splendid

My love is mine

My love is complicated

My love exists in my mind

My love is free

My love is fire

My love fuels my desire

My love is blind

My love is pure

My love is sublime

My love is tender

My love is melodic

My love is special

My love is life

But most importantly

My Love is Love!

No boundaries, no judgments

Just unconditional love

Distance Relationship Woes

I travelled to a distant place

Wanting to see you and kiss your face

But fate played a cruel joke

And it was weeks before we spoke

I was devastated, and my heart broke

I carried on and made the best of the trip

I toured all of greater LA

I didn't let heartbreak stand in my way

I enjoyed West Hollywood and Stana Monica Pier

I saw the stars, the sign, and the Getty's art

I didn't let my sadness and despair tear me apart

I enjoyed museums and the parks

I saw wonders I had only heard about

I saw the city from high above

I saw the maintenance and the ocean

I kept moving forward with so much emotion

I wish it had all been with you

But the memories I made will have to do

If our relationship survives

I hope to be happy with you

If it doesn't, then I will heal

And be grateful for the experience

Hope

I have been stuck for so long

Until I finally believed I belonged

It was rekindling past friendships

That spurred me to positive action

That helped me to finally heal

Helped me to be authentic and truly feel

Helped me to learn to give myself love

Helped me to want and believe I deserve happiness

That led me to finding my partner in you

And wanting a brighter and fuller future

Guided by love, grace and grand adventures

With a woman who displays a pure heart

And I can't wait for our life together to start

Loyal Friendship

You continue to tell me what you see

You talk about me being beautiful and great

And tell me I don't see my own worth

But I think you may be biased

You place me on a pedestal

You see me as someone who is extraordinary

You overestimate my real abilities

Skewing your perception of my reality

I appreciate your fierce loyalty

You are my friend and also my chosen family

But one day, I may fall from my lofty perch

Then you will see my many human flaws

And I will be left bare and raw

I am blessed to have your unconditional love

And I will always extend the same to you

Friendships like ours are far too few

But I need you to see with an unobstructed view

I have learned that I am only human and quite ordinary

That is the me you need to see

But I thank you for always loving me

Christina Saldon

Destiny

Many people don't see the value in gaming

They can't understand the benefits

Not only enhancing our dexterity

But our cognitive abilities

Then there is the social side

That brings us together from far and wide

Different countries, cultures and ways

Giving us opportunities to fill our days

With learning, sharing, and ultimately caring

Friendships are forged during the tapping of the controls

Chosen families are formed

While sharing excitement, laughter and joy

Gaming is not some expensive, trivial toy

It is a gateway to unforeseen happiness

I found some of my best friends through a game called Destiny

I believe we bonded because we were meant to be

Can you see the beauty in the simplistic Irony?

Bad Memories

Traumatic memories used to haunt me day and night

To the point, I couldn't stray from the light

Fear paralyzing me, stirring in me feelings of fright

When sleep did finally come after many sleepless nights

The darkness gave the trauma a voice to speak

Memories consumed my dreams, disturbing my rest

My body was stressed, and I tossed, and I turned

The emotions and fears constantly churned

To be violently awoken from the nightmares

Sweat dripping from my face, leaving my soul bare

Sitting bolt upright, always ready to fight

It takes a few moments to get my head right

Once I realize where I actually am

I flop back down, extremely and utterly exhausted

I close my eyes and try to rub the pain from my head

Reliving the past trauma leaves my heart frosted

Now, the last place I want to be is in this bed

I rise and decide to just get up instead

Afraid to drift back to sleep

Christina Saldon

Fearful the nightmares will return

And more havoc on my soul it will wreak

Now, after much work, my rest is sacred

Memories used to haunt me; now, they are my past

I hope this peace and solace will continue to last

You Can't Save Me

You can't save me. I don't need a saviour

I am a survivor; I need to be the one to save myself

But you can love me like I've never been loved

And you can hold me like I've never been held

You can comfort me when I am struggling and afraid

You can lead me to the light and forgive my mistakes

You can reach out your hand when I need help to rise

You can share your strength when I am too weak to stand

But You can't save me. I don't need a saviour

I am a survivor; I need to be the one to save myself

But you can love me like I've never been loved

And you can hold me like I've never been held

Please just love me like I've never been loved

And you can hold me like I've never been held

But you can't save me. I don't need a saviour

I am a survivor, and I need to save myself

I need to be the one to save myself.

Christina Saldon

Mirror Reframed

Have you ever looked in the mirror

And cringed at what you saw

Had such disdain for your own reflection

With your own voice self, body shaming

Saying you are not pretty enough

That you are ugly and unwanted

That you are unlovable and alone

What trauma did you endure

That made negative self-talk the norm

The mirror is not your enemy

And it is time to see the real you

You are beautiful and strong

The things you used to say were wrong

Do yourself a huge favour

And look at yourself with love

Switch the negative words to positive ones

And allow yourself some grace

Because you belong in this space

Tell yourself you are safe

And you are more than enough.

Now, when you look in the mirror, smile and say

"Hello beautiful, what will we accomplish today!"

Perspective

I used to wonder why I was ever born

Why was I put upon this earth

Just to endure life's many hardships

I saw what was wrong with everything

And thought I was only meant to suffer

Looking for a way to end the pain

Thinking suicide was the answer

But even in my darkest moments

I never took that fatal step

Lots of tears were shed

And I spent many years depressed

Medicated into submission

Trying to find my way to better days

Healing didn't begin until I unlearned the hate speak

Until I learned to love myself

And embrace the good in me and around me

Once I truly took the time to see

I began to heal and feel free from the shackles

That bound me and held me back

Now happiness abounds

I can feel the warmth of life and love

And I want to meet each day

Ready to embrace the good that will come

Perspective, truth, grace, and love are life's true gifts

The Journey

Tiredness weighed me down

My face had a constant frown

Each movement brought so much pain

It left me physically and mentally drained

Chronic pain is very serious

My clouded thoughts were sometimes delirious

Medication is the western world's answer

And I found my depression spreading like a cancer

I spent many decades this way

It wasn't until I began to work on myself

That I could finally feel the brilliance of the sun's rays

And along my healing journey, I found untold wealth

This was my beginning of finding happiness

And now, moving forward, I will accept nothing less

Christina Saldon

Living with Anxiety

Mind constantly racing

Fear crippling

Heart pounding

Breathing laboured

Sweat beading

Face red

Skin burning

Feet firmly planted

Begin deep breathing

Say what you see

Trying to ground

Come back to centre

Anxiety ravages your senses

Draining you, leaving you spent

Exhaustion washing over you

A moment to react

But hours to recover

To feel safe

Another of trauma's unwanted gifts

I have now learned how to gain control quicker

Enabling me to continue on with my day

Freedom's Ride

This must be how the birds feel

As they soar through the air

Feeling the wind on their bodies

And the wonder of everything around them

Clearing the mind of life's clutter

The sound of the bike engine's roar

Seeing everything around you

With nothing to impede your sight

The power under your body

Grounding you and connecting you to nature

To see the mighty Niagara in this way

It was truly spectacular

The natural and furious energy of the falls

The mist as the water hit the bottom

Then rose again, providing us with a shower

Welcomed to combat the day-stifling heat

The sights of the city were something to behold

This trip made better by the company I held

Thank you to my chauffeur

Who took great care of my safety

Ensuring the experience of a lifetime

Such pure joy and freedom

Christina Saldon

The Apology

The impact of your apology

Was far more than your perceived wrong

I know now my ability to finally heal

Came from your words that were so heartfelt

It made my years of hurt begin to melt

Your apology came not just from you

But it became all the apologies I was due

No one had ever apologized for the hurt they caused

No one took responsibility for their part in my pain

Your genuine apology made it possible

For me to begin to heal what once seemed impossible

You helped put me on a path to healing

And this past year has been very revealing

I have learned self-care and self-grace

Allowing myself to exist in a more pleasant space

Now, I fill my days with life's treasures

Embracing all this world has to give

I have truly learned what it means to live

Happiness is now within my grasp

My Phoenix Rising

And I can continue to heal the traumas of the past

Thank you, my dear friend, for the apology

It has given me a renewed energy

My best life is mine to live

And I have so much more to give